MAQĀLĀT

Snippets
of
Sufi Wisdom

PHILIP KRILL

authorHOUSE®

AuthorHouse™
1663 Liberty Drive
Bloomington, IN 47403
www.authorhouse.com
Phone: 833-262-8899

Published by AuthorHouse   12/17/2024

ISBN: 979-8-8230-4037-2 (sc)
ISBN: 979-8-8230-4038-9 (e)

Print information available on the last page.

This book is printed on acid-free paper.

For

The Victims of

Middle Eastern Violence

&

Peace in the Holy Land

I am a hole in the flute that the
Christ's breath moves through ...
listen to this music!

Hafiz

CONTENTS

INTRODUCTION

Sufism is perhaps the deepest mystical current in the rich, venerable and multi-faceted spirituality of Islam. Neither Islam, Judaism, or Christianity must be mistaken simply as 'religion'. All religious practices emerge and develop from a pre-existing apprehension of a Divine Mystery that is too deep for words. *Silence* about God, whose Name is above and beyond every other name, is a cautionary tale told by each of the world's three major religions.

Every religion produces mystics who adhere to the maxim, 'Be still, and know that I am God' (Ps. 46:10). Their experiences of, and writings about, God, tend to run athwart the religious practices, doctrines and everyday understanding of ordinary believers. Mystics are the 'church within the Church' who keep alive a kerygmatic sense of the immediacy of God amidst those for whom religion is but a matter of pious routine.

The Sayings of the Sufi Masters collected in this book[1] are a small sampling of what is a bottomless wealth of Islamic spirituality. The accompanying meditations are my attempt, for a Christian perspective, to disclose a mystic unity underlying the religious differences that so often separate two of the world's greatest faith communities. Like the Persian poet, Hafiz, I aspire to be 'a hole in the flute that the Christ's breath moves through'. The reader can decide how beautiful the music sounds.

17 December 2024
Anniversary of the death of Mevlana Jalaluddin Rumi,

---

[1] All the citations in this book have been taken from *Traveling the Path of Love : Sayings of Sufi Masters*. Inverness, Calif.: Golden Sufi Center. 1995. Llewellyn Vaughan-Lee.

Celestial Journey

The Sufi travels three Journeys - the Journey from God, the Journey to God, and the Journey in God.

TRADITIONAL

MEDITATION

We come from God, and return to God. We are 'gods in God' since 'before the foundation of the world' (Eph. 1:4).

PRAYER

Awaken us to our divinely human identity, O God. Show us that *in* You 'we live and move and have our being' (Acts 17:28).

Chicken or Egg?

How we see God is a direct reflection of how we see ourselves. If God brings to mind mostly fear and blame, it means there is too much fear and blame welled inside us. If we see God as full of love and compassion, so are we.

SHAMS-I TABRÎZ

MEDITATION

We see God *as we are*, not as God is. 'God is love, and those who abide in love abide in God' (1 Jn. 4:16). If we know God, we know love; if we know love, we know God.

PRAYER

You have shown us that love alone is credible, O God. Purify our hearts with Your love, so we may 'see with what love You have given us' (1 Jn. 3:1), and with what love we can love others (Jn. 15:12).

Divine Empowerment

No one by himself can find the Path to Him. Whoever goes to His street goes with His feet.

MAGHRIBÍ

MEDITATION

God is 'the Way, the Truth and the Life' (Jn. 15:15). If we desire union with God, it is only because God desires intimacy with us.

PRAYER

Grant us holy desire, O God. Show us that You are 'at work in us, both to will and to accomplish Your good pleasure' (Phil. 2:13).

Run, Don't Walk

If you walk toward Him, He comes to you running.

HADÎTH

MEDITATION

God is never outdone in generosity. Our desire for God is a sign of God's desire to share His Life with us.

PRAYER

Fill us with holy desire, O God. Show us that our desire for You is a participation in Your desire for us.

One Step at a Time

Take one step away from yourself and - behold! - the Path!

ABÚ SAʿÎD IBN ABÍ-L-KHAYR

MEDITATION

In a single act of self-transcendence, we enter the kingdom of God. The slightest movement of self-forgetfulness transports us instantly to God's right hand.

PRAYER

Usher us into the mystical space of self-transcendence, O God. Show us that self-forgetfulness is the path to self-fulfillment.

The New Jerusalem

When you seek God, seek Him in your heart - He is not in Jerusalem, nor in Mecca, nor in the hajj.

YÛNUS EMRE

MEDITATION

Every person is a dwelling place of God. Discovering God within, we find 'the pearl of great price' (Mt. 13:46).

PRAYER

Direct our attention inward, O God. Show us You are found 'not in the earthquake, the firestorm or the tornado, but in the small, still Voice' within (1 Kg. 19:11-12).

Sacred Jealousy

Between me and You, there is only me. Take away the me, so only You remain.

AL-HALLÂJ

MEDITATION

Self-aggrandizement impedes our deification. Self-surrender gives God permission to be our 'all in all' (1 Cor. 15:28).

PRAYER

Empty us of ego, and fill us with Your divine Presence, O God. Destroy our self-interest and permeate us with Your deifying grace.

Mystic Mindfulness

The perfect mystic is not an ecstatic devotee lost in contemplation of Oneness, nor a saintly recluse shunning all commerce with mankind, but 'the true saint' goes in and out amongst the people and eats and sleeps with them and buys and sells in the market and marries and takes part in social intercourse, and never forgets God for a single moment.

ABÛ SAÎD IBN ABÎ-L-KHAYR

MEDITATION

Mystics are contemplatives in action. Mystics behold God in every person they meet, and see the world as a theophany of God's creative Love.

PRAYER

Grant us a deified vision, O God. Open the eyes of our hearts to apprehend the world as permeated by Your divine Presence.

Fallen Fruit

Everything in the world of existence has an end and a goal. The end is maturity and the goal is freedom. For example, fruit grows on the tree until it is ripe and then falls. The ripened fruit represents maturity, and the fallen fruit, freedom. The final goal is returning to one's origin. Everything which reaches its origin has reached its goal. A farmer sows grain in the ground and tends it. It begins to grow, eventually seeds, and again becomes grain. It has returned to its original form. The circle is complete. Completing the circle of existence is freedom.

NASAFÎ

MEDITATION

The End is in the beginning, and the beginning is in the End. Nothing comes from God that does not return to God without having accomplished the End for which it began (Isa. 55:11).

PRAYER

Set us free with divine freedom, O God (Rom. 8:21). Bring to perfection what You desired for us from the beginning.

Been There Before

I was asked, 'What is the end of the mystic?' I answered, 'When he is as he was where he was before he was.'

DHŪ-L-NŪN

MEDITATION

Our true identity is eternally established in, and by, God. God knows us 'before we were formed in our mother's womb' (Jer. 1:5).

PRAYER

Help us to know ourselves as we are known by You, O God (1 Cor. 13:12). Reveal the name 'which no one knows except the one who receives it' (Rev. 2:17).

Guru Within

Then there arises the question of how to find the real guru ... The real teacher is within, the lover of reality is one's own sincere self, and if one is really seeking truth, sooner or later one will certainly find a true teacher.

INAYAT KHAN

MEDITATION

'When the student is ready, the teacher appears' (Lao Tzu). God's timing is always perfect.

PRAYER

Reveal Your divine synchronicity, O God. Show us that 'all things work for good in the lives of those' who surrender to You completely (Rom. 8:28; 2 Cor. 9:8).

Prophetic Parallel

The spiritual master is to his community what the prophet is to his nation.

ABÛ SA'ÎD IBN ABÎ-L-KHAYR

MEDITATION

Divine illumination comes from above. Spiritual revelation shatters the status quo.

PRAYER

Show us that 'what is born of the flesh is flesh, and what is born of the Spirit is spirit', O God (Jn. 3:6). Teach us to 'set our minds on things that are above, not on things that are below' (Col. 3:2).

Follow Your Heart

The path to the Truth is a labor of the heart, not of the head. Make your heart your primary guide! Not your mind.

SHAMS-I TABRÎZ

MEDITATION

Thinking cannot solve the problems thinking creates. The Wisdom of the heart is to the knowledge of the mind what the rising sun is to the melting mist.

PRAYER

Illumine our hearts with Your uncreated Light, O God. Draw us into the luminous darkness where true enlightenment is found.

Go With the Flow

Saints are like rivers, they flow where they are directed ... Saints have to do things the people will misjudge, and which from the worldly point of view could be condemned, because the world judges by appearances ... A Saint is beyond good and evil, but Saints are people of the highest morality and will never give a bad example.

BHAI SAHIB

MEDITATION

Saints experience a dissolution of the deliberative (*gnomic*) will. They learn to do the truth co-naturally and become virtually incapable of making a mistake.

PRAYER

Grant us the virtuosity of the saints, O God. Show us intuitively the right thing to do, and say, in every situation.

All In

The saints of God are known by three signs: their thought is of God, their dwelling is in God, and their business is with God.

MA'RÛF AL-KARKHÎ

MEDITATION

Saints 'live and move and have their being' in God (Acts 17:28). We do too, but, unlike the saints, we often don't realize it.

PRAYER

Awaken us to our true identity as 'gods in God,' O God. Show us that You are the Goal of our desires, and the Source of our aspirations.

Want for Nothing

Last night my teacher taught me the lesson of poverty: having nothing and wanting nothing.

RÛMÎ

MEDITATION

Total detachment means perfect freedom. When we desire nothing but God, the world is our oyster.

PRAYER

Grant us the grace of complete surrender, O God. Show us that 'letting go' is the key to 'having all'.

The Only True Guide

The only guide to God is God Himself.

KALÂBÂDHÎ

MEDITATION

God is the the Way, the Truth, and the Life (Jn. 14:6). All the way to heaven *is* heaven.

PRAYER

Guide us into Your supernal glory, O God. Show us that '[T]he end of all our exploring will be to arrive where we started, and know the place for the first time' (T. S. Eliot, *Little Gidding*).

Holy Abandonment

Intellect is always cautious and advises, 'Beware too much ecstasy', whereas love says, 'Oh, never mind! Take the plunge!'

SHAMS-I TABRÎZ

MEDITATION

Holy abandonment is *of God*. The Father 'abandons himself' in begetting his Word, and the Word 'abandons himself' by pouring out his Spirit.

PRAYER

Grant us divine abandonment, O God. Transmute our 'fear of abandonment' into abandonment as 'trustful surrender'.

Holy Desire

Oh Lord, nourish me not with love but with the desire for love.

IBN 'ARABÎ

MEDITATION

Our desire for love is the Presence of God within us, drawing us to Himself as the Fullness of Love (1 Jn. 4:8).

PRAYER

Quench our thirst for love, O God! 'As the deer longs for flowing streams, so our souls long for You' (Ps. 42:1).

Love's True Measure

*Longing is a state of commotion in the heart hoping for meeting with the Beloved.
The depth of longing is commensurate with the servant's love of God.*

AL-QUSHAYRÍ

MEDITATION

Holy desire is the soul of sanctity. It's not what we *achieve* that matters,
but the *earnestness with which* we seek the One who loves us (1 Jn. 4:10).

PRAYER

Grant us ever-increasing desire for You, O God. Show us that our
longing for You is never outdone by Your desire *for us*.

Waiting on God

God, when He created the world, had created no creatures in it; and if He had filled it full of millet from East to West and from earth to heaven; and if then He had created one bird and bidden it eat one grain of this millet every thousand years, and if, after that, He had created a man and kindled in his heart this mystic longing and had told him that he would never win to his goal until this bird left not a single millet-seed in the whole world, and that he would continue until then in this burning pain of love - It would still be a thing soon ended!

TRADITIONAL

MEDITATION

The desire for God is an eternal Flame burning in the Sufi's (saint's) heart. This Flame is not easily - or ever - extinguished.

PRAYER

Fill us with holy desire, O God. Keep the flame of Your love burning within us to the point of consummation.

Source of All Desire

The inner truth of desire is that it is a restive motion in the heart in search of God.

AL-QUSHAYRÎ

MEDITATION

All movements of the heart - even those towards objects unworthy of our love - are, at bottom, aspirations for God.

PRAYER

Show us that, in desiring anything, we are desiring You, O God. Show us that You are the transcendental *Telos* (aim, goal) of all our temporal yearnings.

He Loved Us First

Until the beam of His love shines out to guide the soul, it does not set out to behold the love of His Face. My heart feels not the slightest attraction towards Him until an attraction comes from Him and works upon my heart. Since I learnt that He longs for me, longing for Him never leaves me for an instant.

MAGHRIBÎ

MEDITATION

Our longings for God are by-products of God's longing for us. Appreciating the prevenient love of God is the key that unlocks true love for God.

PRAYER

Show us that it is not we who have loved You, but that You have loved us first, O God (1 Jn. 4:10, 19). Humble us with the awareness that Your love for us makes possible our love for You.

Omnipresent

You can study God through everything and everyone in the universe because God is not confined in a mosque, synagogue, or church.

SHAMS-I TABRÎZ

MEDITATION

There is nowhere God is not found, yet God cannot be found as other things are found. The world is in God, and God is in the world, but the world is not God, and God is not the world.

PRAYER

Touch us with Your veiled Presence, O God. Help us to see and love You in all things, and to see and love all things in You.

'I Thirst'

Not only the thirsty seek the water, the water as well seeks the thirsty.

RŪMĪ

MEDITATION

God's 'thirst' is to satisfy ours. God creates us as thirsty creatures so that, in our weakness, we will drink deeply of His life-giving water.

PRAYER

Teach us the meaning of Your words, 'I thirst' (Jn. 4:7-14; 19:28), O God. Show us that whoever drinks of the water that You 'shall give will never thirst', and that 'this water will become in him a spring of water welling up to eternal life' (Jn 4:14).

Consuming Fire

Spiritual need is a living and luminous fire placed by God in the breasts of His servants that their 'self' (nafs, or ego) may be burned; and when it has been burned, this fire becomes the fire of 'longing' (shawq) which never dies, neither in this world nor in the next.

ABÛ SA'ÎD IBN ABÎ-L-KHAYR

MEDITATION

'Our God is a consuming fire' (Heb. 12:19) that purifies all human desires. Purged of possessiveness, our desire for God becomes the sum and substance of sanctity.

PRAYER

Reveal Yourself as the Source and Satisfaction of all desire, O God. Purify our desires of all but Your divinity.

Divine Intimacy

It is He who suffers His absence in me, Who through me cries out to Himself.
Love's most strange, most holy mystery - we are intimate beyond belief.

RÛMÎ

MEDITATION

In loving us, God loves Himself, *in* and *through* us. Our very existence
is an expression of, and intimacy with, the One who gives us life.

PRAYER

Show that 'in You, we live and move and have our being', O God
(Acts 17:28). Show us that we are *who* we are, and *as* we are, because
of Who You Are (Ex. 3:14).

God's Gratitude

Before He created them, He praised them; before they glorify Him, He gave them thanks.

AL-HALLÁJ

MEDITATION

God's glory is the human person fully alive (St. Irenaeus). When we are filled with joy, God's joy is made complete (Jn. 15:11).

PRAYER

Awaken us to Your delight in dwelling in our company, O God (Rev. 21:3). Show us that Your great pleasure is to share Your joy with us (Jn. 16:24).

God Alone

God, if I worship Thee in fear of Hell, burn me in Hell; and if I worship Thee in hope of Paradise, exclude me from Paradise; but if I worship Thee for Thine own sake, withhold not Thine everlasting beauty.

RÁBI'A

MEDITATION

Love of God is its own reward. Our love for God is perfect when we love God for Who God is, not for what God does.

PRAYER

Strip us of ulterior reasons to prefer You, O God. Grant us the grace to 'choose the one thing necessary' (Lk. 10:42) for no other reason than it's You.

Too Deep for Words

And if I send Thee greetings, Thou art the greeting, and if I speak, Thou art the prayer.

MAGHRIBÎ

MEDITATION

God works within us, both for the desire and the accomplishment of any good that we do (Phil. 2:13). Our desire for God is a gift of God's own Spirit.

PRAYER

Awaken us to the pre-eminence of Your Presence in our lives, O God. Show us that You, who are within us, 'are greater than he who is in the world' (1 Jn. 4:4).

In Us as Us

The eyes which regard God are also the eyes through which He regards the world.

TRADITIONAL

MEDITATION

In God's Light, we see light (Ps. 36:9). Illumined by God's uncreated Light, we regard the entire world with love.

PRAYER

Remind us that we see the world as we are, not as it is, O God. Purify our hearts such that we behold all things bathed in Your benevolence.

Transfiguration

What predominates in the heart of the mystic while he is at prayer is his sense of the mystery of Him in Whose Presence he stands ... until he has finished praying and departs with a face so changed that his friends would not recognize him, because of the awe that he feels at the Majesty of God.

MUHÂSIBÎ

MEDITATION

Divinization results from abiding contemplatively with God. Like Moses, we emerge from contemplative prayer with countenances transfigured (Ex. 34:35).

PRAYER

Deepen our contemplative stillness, O God. Increase our intimacy with You to the point of deification.

Luminous Darkness

How is it that those people are most beautiful who pray at night? Because they are alone with the All-Merciful who covers them with light from His light.

HASAN IBN 'ALÎ

MEDITATION

The darkness is luminous for those who behold God with their inner eye. God is the Luminous Darkness from which all other lights emerge.

PRAYER

Draw us into Your luminous darkness, O God. Inspire us to abide with You in contemplative silence.

Tied in 'Not's'

Intellect and love are made of different materials. Intellect ties people in knots and risks nothing, but love dissolves all tangles and risks everything.

SHAMS-I TABRÎZ

MEDITATION

Love is a divine solvent that dissolves every barrier and loosens every knot. There is no 'Not' in God, - 'for the Son of God was not Yes and No, but in Him it is always Yes' (2 Cor. 1:19).

PRAYER

Show us that in You 'there is no darkness,' O God. Illumine us with Your uncreated Light in which our conundrums and misgivings are revealed as illusions.

Inverse Intentionality

Worship God in such a way that you see Him. If you cannot do so, be aware that He sees you.

AL-GHAZZÂLÎ

MEDITATION

'The eye with which we see God is the eye with which God sees us' (Meister Eckhart). Prayer is an exercise in 'inverse intentionality' where we find God beholding us in love *before* we turn our gaze towards Him.

PRAYER

Make us aware of Your prevenient Gaze, O God. Show us that 'noticing You noticing us' is the mystery of contemplative prayer.

Apprehending the Non-existent God

Become silent and go by the way of silence towards non-existence. And when you become non-existent you will be all praise and all laud.

RÛMÎ

MEDITATION

The culmination of holiness is *kenosis* (self-emptying). 'Those who humble themselves will be exalted, and all who exalt themselves will be humbled' (Lk. 14:11).

PRAYER

Show us that both the apogee and nadir of sanctity are humility, O God. Show us that, with You, poverty is wealth, and wealth is poverty.

Be Still and Know

I went to see my friend. I saw him sitting in meditation, so motionless that not even one hair moved. I asked, 'From whom did you learn such deep meditation?' 'I learned it from a cat waiting by a mouse hole. The cat was much stiller than I.'

AL-SHÍBLÍ

MEDITATION

Our pets live completely in the present moment. We could learn a lot from cats and dogs.

PRAYER

Grant us the blessed unselfconsciousness of household pets, O God. Show us how to 'be still and know' You are God (Ps. 46:10).

Power of the Now

The best act of worship is watchfulness of the moments. The servant must not look beyond his limit, not contemplate anything other than his Lord, and not associate with anything other than his present moment.

ABŪ BAKR MUHAMMAD AL-WĀSITĪ

MEDITATION

The greatest sacrament is that of the present moment. When we experience God as the 'Power of Now', we have found 'the pearl of great price' (Mt. 13:46).

PRAYER

Awaken us to Your Presence in the Eternal Now, O God. Remind us that You can never be found other than in the present moment, since it is never not Now.

Divine Openness

Sâlih al-Murrî said, 'Whoever is persistent in knocking at the door is on the verge of having it opened for him.' Râb'ia asked him, 'When was the door closed so that one had to ask to have it opened?'

SÁLIH AL-MURRÎ

MEDITATION

The gates of Paradise are never closed. We lock ourselves out whenever we imagine otherwise.

PRAYER

Disabuse us of our need to cajole You, O God. Show us the folly that we could ever be excluded from Your divinizing Love.

Blessed Exhaustion

You imagined that you would accomplish this task through your own strength, activity, and effort ...However, when you travel this road until your legs are exhausted and you fall down flat, until you have no more strength to move forward, then God's grace will take you in its arms.

RÛMÎ

MEDITATION

Breakdown often precedes breakthrough. When our projects of self-sanctification collapse, our spiritual transformation begins.

PRAYER

Grant us the grace of religious failure, O God. Destroy our efforts at pious self-aggrandizement, and transfigure us to be 'the praise of Your glory' (Eph. 1:12).

Ecstatic Nothingness

A bedouin was asked, 'Do you acknowledge the Lord?' He replied, 'How could I not acknowledge Him who has sent me hunger, made me naked and impoverished, and caused me to wander from country to country?' As he spoke thus, he entered a state of ecstasy.

ABÛ SA'ÎD IBN ABÎ-L-KHAYR

MEDITATION

God divests us of ourselves so that, as wandering pilgrims, we will cast our cares on Him alone.

PRAYER

Make us spiritual bedouins, O God. Show us that we have no lasting home other than within Your Heart of infinite Love.

Free Indeed!

Someone asked Junayd: 'Slave of God who yet are free, tell me how to reach a state of contentment.' Junayd replied: 'When one has learned through love to accept.'

AL-JUNAYD

MEDITATION

Acceptance is the answer to all our problems today. Acceptance, without resentment, is the key that unlocks the Kingdom of God.

PRAYER

Reveal acceptance as the 'narrow way' (Mt. 7:14) leading to peace, O God. Show us that Your Kingdom 'is within' our every act of acceptance (Lk. 17:21)

Die Before You Die

When you die of surrender, only then you will live forever. If you are put to death through surrender, there is no such thing as death for you, for you have died already.

PERSIAN POEM

MEDITATION

Die before you die: this is the mystic wisdom of the ages. Letting go, we are lifted up, and surrendering our self-interest, we experience self-fulfillment.

PRAYER

Grant us the grace of joyful acceptance, O God. Show us that surrender is the way to victory in Your kingdom.

Love Beyond Words

Most of problems of the world stem from linguistic mistakes and simple misunderstanding. Don't ever take words at face value. When you step into the zone of love, language, as we know it becomes obsolete.

SHAMS-I TABRÎZ

MEDITATION

Reading about water is not the same as drinking it. Learning about God is not the same as knowing God.

PRAYER

Slake our thirst for love with Your living water, O God (Jn. 7:38). Satisfy our spiritual hunger with 'the bread come down from heaven' (Jn. 6:50-51).

With Empty Hands

I offer to Thee the only thing I have - my capacity of being filled with Thee.

ANONYMOUS

MEDITATION

We are a 'holy emptiness' inviting the in-filling of God. We are virginal souls created for ecstatic communion with our Divine Spouse (2 Cor. 11:2).

PRAYER

Penetrate us with Your divinizing Love, O God. Permeate us with an ecstatic infusion of Your glorious Life.

Go Figure

Surrender is the most difficult thing in the world while you are doing it, and the easiest when it is done.

BHAI SAHIB

MEDITATION

When the pain of holding on becomes greater than the pain of letting go, we let go. Why not do this *willingly* before the suffering becomes too great?

PRAYER

Grant us the grace of willing surrender, O God. Show us that our true joy means allowing You to accomplish Your desire (will) within us.

Divine GPS

Do you think I know what I'm doing? That for one breath or half a breath I belong to myself? As much as a pen knows what it's writing, or the ball can guess where it's going next.

RÚMÍ

MEDITATION

'Can the axe vaunt itself over the one who hews with it? Can the rod wield the one who lifts it' (Isa. 10:15)? Less so can we compel the God who made us for His glory.

PRAYER

Forgive us for 'babbling on like the pagans' in prayer, O God (Mt. 6:7). Teach us that silent surrender to You in contemplation is the heart and soul of sanctity.

Purity of Heart

Purity of the heart is to will one thing.

TRADITIONAL

MEDITATION

Devotion is deleterious if not singular in focus. Contemplative prayer is 'the one thing necessary' that 'will not be taken' from those who embrace it (Lk. 10:42).

PRAYER

Teach us to separate the 'trivial many' from the 'vital few' in our devotion to You, O God. Keep us centered on the two great commandments, i.e., love of You above all things, and love of our neighbor as ourselves (Mt. 22:40).

True Desire

God said to me, 'What do you desire?' I replied, 'I desire not to desire.'

BÁYEZÍD BISTÁMÍ

MEDITATION

God is the Source and Satisfaction of our every desire. To desire what God desires is the one thing desirable.

PRAYER

Teach us to desire as You desire, O God. Show us that Your desire for our eternal joy is the fulfillment of all desire - both Yours and ours.

Acquiring the Character of God

The meaning of noble character is that the harshness of men does not affect you once you have become attentive to God.

AL-HALLÂJ

MEDITATION

Awareness of God's Presence is the antidote to every anxiety. The practice of the Presence of God 'makes all things new' (Rev. 21:5).

PRAYER

Teach us how to be in the place of shame without resentment, O God. Show us that unlimited forgiveness (Mt. 18:22) occurs naturally when we abide in Your Presence.

God's Light Within

God placed within the heart knowledge of Him and so the heart became lit by God's Light. By this light He gave the heart eyes to see.

AL-HAKÎM AT-TIRMIDHÎ

MEDITATION

In God's light, we see light (Ps. 36:9). Enlightenment (salvation) begins when we apprehend God as the Source of our interior illuminations.

PRAYER

Show us that the world is backlit by the Light of Your Face, O God. Show us that You are the uncreated Light illuminating both our hearts and the heavens.

Light Merging with Light

Each time a light rises up from you, a light comes down towards you .... it is the light in Heaven which yearns for you and is attracted to your light, and descends towards you. This is the secret of the mystical journey.

NAJM AL-DÍN KUBRÁ

MEDITATION

God is the 'Living Flame of Love' (St. John of the Cross), setting our hearts aflame with His burning Presence. Our love for God is a by-product of God's Fire within.

PRAYER

Enflame us with Your purifying Presence, O God. Show us that our passion for You is the heat radiating from Your divine Fire within us.

Light upon Light

My heart is light upon light, a beautiful Mary with Jesus in the womb.

RÚMÍ

MEDITATION

Nothing compares with a mother's love, especially when the mother's child is God. We are all 'mothers of God' when we conceive of God's Light within (Mk. 3:35).

PRAYER

Awaken us to Your Presence within us, O God. Show us that the love we have for You is You Yourself, desiring to be born in us.

Ecstasy

True ecstasy is the conjunction of light with light, when the soul of man meets the Divine Light.

'ABDU'L-QÂDIR AL-GÎLÂNÎ

MEDITATION

Deification occurs when we can honestly say 'It is no longer we who live, but God who lives in us' (Gal. 2:20). Merging with God's Light, we become 'partakers of God's divine nature' (2 Pt. 1:4).

PRAYER

Grant us the ecstasy of merging with Your divine Light, O God. Make us one with You - without confusion - in a synergy of bliss-filled divinization.

The Divine Mirror

By means of the Divine Light, the heart becomes polished so that it shines like a polished mirror ... when it is polished and shining, it beholds the Realm of Divine Glory, and the Divine Glory becomes revealed to it.

AL-HAKÎM AT-TIRMIDHÎ

MEDITATION

We are created to reflect the infinite glory of God. Divine luminosity radiates from a perfectly polished soul.

PRAYER

Make us ever-better mirrors of Your divine splendor, O God. Polish the mirrors of our hearts so we can become the praise of Your Divine Glory (Eph. 1:12-14).

God's Self-Revelation

God is necessary to us in order that we may exist, while we are necessary to Him in order that He may be manifested to Himself. I also give Him life by knowing Him in my heart.

IBN 'ARABÎ

MEDITATION

Though utterly transcendent, and needing us for nothing, it has nevertheless pleased God to create us so that God may manifest Himself in us, through us, and (if we can believe it!) *as* us.

PRAYER

Awaken us to our divine dignity as finite emanations of Your ineffable Presence, O God. Show us that we are 'gods by grace', just as You are God by nature.

Who Is Seeking Whom?

Not a single lover would seek union if the Beloved were not seeking it.

RÚMÍ

MEDITATION

All love begins and ends in God. Our desire for communion with others is a function of God's desire for communion with us.

PRAYER

Show us that every human love is a reflection of You loving Yourself in and through us, O God. Reveal Yourself to be the Source and Satisfaction of our every love.

Divine Intimacy

I am nearer to you than you are to yourself.

RÛMÎ

Meditation

God is the Inside of our inside and the Outside of our outside.
Nothing exists apart from God, even though God is absolutely
independent of all that is.

Prayer

Reveal our mystical participation in Your divine nature, O God (2
Pt. 1:4). Show us that we are one with You in an asymmetrical co-
inherence of Love.

Absence as Presence

He hides His presence from you, it is because He is listening to you.

AL-HALLĀJ

MEDITATION

Listening is an act of *kenosis* (self-forgetfulness) in which the listener is silently present. God's apparent silence is a manifestation of His listening Presence.

PRAYER

Remind us that no prayer goes unheard, O God. Draw us into Your listening silence, and show us that You are supremely present in Your apparent absence.

Containing God

My earth and My heaven contains Me not, but the heart of My faithful servant contains Me.

HADÎTH QUDSÎ

MEDITATION

We are, by God's grace, the 'dwelling place' of God (Eph. 2:22). Though far above the heavens, it has pleased God to 'pitch his tent' in the hearts of every human person.

PRAYER

Reveal our divine dignity as living temples of Your divine Presence, O God. Open our hearts so You can take up Your home within us (Rev. 3:20).

Intercourse Divine

The love of God in its essence is really the illumination of the heart by joy because of its nearness to the Beloved ... the joy of that intercourse overwhelms the mind, so that it is no longer concerned with this world and what is therein.

MUHÁSIBÍ

MEDITATION

Knowledge of God in the heart is an act of mystical intercourse, of which the ecstasy of sexual delight is but a dim intimation.

PRAYER

Unite us to Yourself in an act of ecstatic intimacy, O God. Fill us with the joy of 'knowing' You in the fullest, nuptial meaning of the word (Gen. 4:1).

Divine Elixir

God has a wine for His friends, such that when they drink of it, they become intoxicated, and once they are intoxicated they become merry, and once they are merry, they become purged, and once they are purged they become melted down, and once they are melted down, they become purified, and once they become purified they arrive, and once they arrive they become united with the Divine, and once they are united with the Divine there is no distinction between them and their Beloved.

HADÎTH QUDSÎ

MEDITATION

Spirituality is the pursuit of divine intoxication. Intoxicated by His Spirit, we dissolve into God's Embrace.

PRAYER

Grant us spiritual intoxication, O God. Dissolve our religious inhibitions, and grant us an insatiable craving for Your divine Elixir.

Consubstantial

The being of the lover and Beloved are the same.

SHÁH NI'MATOLLÁH

MEDITATION

God is Love (1 Jn. 4:8), and we are 'love from Love'. God alone is God, and we are 'gods in God'.

PRAYER

Show us that our very existence is an expression of You as Love, O God. Show us that we are begotten by You (1 Jn. 5:18) to become the 'praise of Your glory' (Eph. 1:12-14).

Unveiled

Between the lover and the Beloved, there must be no veil. Thou thyself art thine own veil - get out of the way!

HÂFIZ

MEDITATION

The head is often blind to what is intuitively known by the heart. 'The heart has its reasons which reason knows nothing of' (Paschal).

PRAYER

Tear the veil of our sweet encounter with You, O God. Dissolve the thoughts that impede our heartfelt union with You.

Beyond Enjoyment

The servant's love for God is a state too subtle for words ... Describing the lover as annihilated in the Beloved is more fitting than describing him as having enjoyment of Him.

AL-QUSHAYRÍ

MEDITATION

Love has the power to dissolve. Our knees grow weak, and our hearts melt, when we encounter the beloved.

PRAYER

Anneal us in the furnace of Your divine Love, O God. Dissolve us in the cauldron of Your Embrace, and purify our hearts as 'gold tested by fire' (1 Pt. 1:7).

Divine Alchemy

Love means that the attributes of the lover are changed into those of the Beloved.

AL-JUNAYD

MEDITATION

'God became man so man could become God' (St. Athanasius). God's Midas touch turns our hearts of lead into hearts of gold.

PRAYER

Transform our hearts of stone into hearts of flesh (Ezk. 11:19), O God. Work Your divine alchemy so we may become 'partakers of Your divine nature' (2 Pt. 1:4).

Divine Diminishment

The true lover finds the light only if, like the candle, he is his own fuel, consuming himself.

'ATTÂR

MEDITATION

For those who love, self-dispossession is self-fulfillment. No greater love have we than to give ourselves for the sake of the beloved (Jn. 15:13).

PRAYER

Grant us the grace of radical self-donation, O God. Remind us that 'the measure we give will be the measure given back' to us (Lk. 6:38).

Endless Love

When the world pushes you to your knees, you're in the perfect position to pray.

RUMI

MEDITATION

Nothing happens by chance. The world itself conspires to bring us to our knees so that God can raise us up in glory.

PRAYER

Show us that every impediment is an invitation to divine relinquishment, O God. Show us that obstacles are opportunities for greater surrender to You.

Passio > Ratio

Love is represented by fire, and reason by smoke. When love comes, reason disappears. Reason cannot live with the folly of love; love has nothing to do with human reason.

'ATTÁR

MEDITATION

Love makes fools of us all. Better to be a fool for love than wise in the ways of mammon (Lk. 9:10-13).

PRAYER

Grant us the smoke-less Fire of Your divine Mercy, O God. Enflame us with Your unreasonable Love.

Fire of Love

Call me, and though hell-fire lie between, my love will make it easy to pass through the flames.

ABÛ SA'ÎD IBN ABÎ-L-KHAYR

MEDITATION

Like a mother rushing into a burning building to save her child, the lover of God will go through hell to find the Beloved.

PRAYER

Call us, and we will go through hell to answer Your summons, O God. The moment we hear the sound of Your voice, all within us leaps for joy (Lk. 1:44).

Celestial Journey

Loneliness and solitude are two different things. When you are lonely, it is easy to delude yourself into believing that you are on the right path. Solitude is better for us, as it means being alone without feeling lonely.

SHAMS-I TABRÍZ

MEDITATION

Solitude transforms loneliness into love. Absence makes the heart grow fonder in the spiritually mature.

PRAYER

We are never less alone than when resting in You, O God (Mt. 11:28). Grant us the grace of abiding with You in the solitude of our hearts.

Love Beyond Love

A thing can be explained only by what is more subtle than itself; there is nothing subtler than love: by what then shall love be explained?

SUMNÛN

MEDITATION

Love, like God, is self-explanatory. Where love is present, there is no need to gild the lily.

PRAYER

'God is love, and those who abide in love abide in God, and God abides in them' (1 Jn. 4:16). Divinize us with Your omnipresent Love, O God.

Hearts Aflame

Love is a fire in the heart that burns up all but the Beloved's wishes.

TRADITIONAL

MEDITATION

'God is a consuming fire' (Heb. 12:29), vaporizing our sins as so much dross (1 Cor. 3:15), making our hearts incandescent with divine Love.

PRAYER

Enflame us with Your transfiguring Love, O God. Incinerate our sins so our hearts may be set aglow with Your divine glory.

True Knowledge

True knowledge is what is unveiled in hearts.

TRADITIONAL

MEDITATION

God speaks with 'sighs too deep for words' (Rom. 8:26). It is in the heart that we can 'be still and know' that God is God (Ps. 46:10).

PRAYER

Attune us to the Inner Voice, O God. Show us that only in the heart can we hear the whispers of Your Spirit.

To Know is to Love,
To Love is to Know

To know God is to love Him.

ANONYMOUS

MEDITATION

Freedom and necessity are identical in God, as well as in those who 'know' God. Just as God cannot *not* love, those who know God cannot *not* love Him completely.

PRAYER

Remove all questions about loving You, O God. Show us that we have no choice *but* to love You once the glory of Your Face is unveiled.

Unveiled Vision

Love leads to knowledge of the Divine mysteries. Those who love and abide in God ... are given a vision of God unveiled, and they see Him with the eye of certainty.

'AMR IBN 'UTHMÁN AL-MAKKÍ

MEDITATION

We cannot comprehend God with our mind, but we can apprehend God with our love. Those 'grasped' by the love of God are given a vision of God that divinizes them.

PRAYER

Grant us the grace to behold You face-to-face, O God. Like Moses, may we emerge from our encounter with You with faces iridescent with divine glory (Ex. 34:35).

Treasure Houses of God

The mystics are the treasure houses of God. God deposits in them the knowledge of mysteries and information concerning wonderful things, and they speak of them with the tongue of eternity and interpret them with an interpretation that is everlasting.

ABU SA'ID AL-KHARAZ

MEDITATION

The imagination of the mystic exceeds the cleverness of the intellectual. Saints understand that 'the foolishness of God is wiser than men, and the weakness of God is stronger than men' (1 Cor. 1:25).

PRAYER

Grant us to penetrate the mystical meaning of our religious routines, O God. Inspire us to 'live according to the Spirit and set our minds on the things of the Spirit' (Rom. 8:5).

Purity

True knowledge of God is gained when the lover comes in contact with the Beloved through secret communion with Him.

ANONYMOUS

MEDITATION

Prayer is an event of intimate, holy communion with God. True knowledge of God is an experience of transfiguration, not a commercial transaction.

PRAYER

Draw us into Your divine Embrace, O God. Grant us the ecstasy of nuptial communion with You.

The Heart of the Matter

When God wishes to conquer a heart, He entrusts it with secrets, which the heart then perceives and proclaims.

AL-HALLAJ

MEDITATION

What we hear in secret, we are compelled to preach from the rooftops (Lk. 12:3). Knowing God, how can we keep from singing?

PRAYER

Fill us to overflowing with Your inspiration, O God. Make us living words of Your unspeakable Goodness.

Taste and See

He who tastes, knows.

ANONYMOUS

MEDITATION

'Taste and see the goodness of the Lord' (Ps. 34:8). It is those who 'feed on God' who enjoy eternal life (Jn. 6:54).

PRAYER

Give us Your flesh to eat and Your blood to drink, O God (Jn. 6:53). Show that when we feed on You, we have 'already passed from death to life' (Jn. 5:24).

'SELF' Knowledge

Who knows himself, knows his Lord.

HADITH

MEDITATION

God is the Self within the self. In God 'we live and move and have
our identity' (Acts 17:28). Only in heaven will we know ourselves as
God knows us (1 Cor. 13:12; Rev. 2:13).

PRAYER

Show us that knowledge of ourselves is inseparable from knowing
You, O God. Show us that to know ourselves, we must know You,
and, knowing You, we know ourselves.

Advaita?

When you know yourself, your 'I-ness' vanishes, and you know that you and God are one and the same.

IBN 'ARABÎ

MEDITATION

We are in God, and God is in us, but we are not God, and God is not us. Our existence is a participation in the Unparticipatable God.

PRAYER

Show us that our 'lives are hidden' in You, O God (Col. 3:3). Show us that our deepest identity is rooted in You as the Great 'I AM' (Ex. 3:14).

Abide with Me

Nothing sees God and dies, even as nothing sees God and lives, because His life is everlasting, and he who sees Him, remains in Him, and is made everlasting.

ABU NU'AYM AL-ISFAHĀNI

MEDITATION

To know God is to love God, and to love God is to see God. Apprehending God as the Beginning (*Alpha*) and End (*Omega*) of our existence imparts eternal life.

PRAYER

'Blessed are those who walk in the light of your countenance', O God (Ps. 89:15). Basking in Your Presence, we are deified by Your eternal glory.

Third Eye

When. the mystic's spiritual eye is opened, his physical eye is closed, and he sees nothing but God.

ABÛ SULAYMÂN AD-DÂRÂNÎ

MEDITATION

God is the unseen Horizon within which our human experience happens. We are not human beings having a spiritual experience, but spiritual beings having a human experience.

PRAYER

Open our inner eye to Your unseen Presence, O God. Grant us an interior vision of Your Infinity which sharpens the focus of our earthly perceptions.

Beyond Imagination

When you imagine God, God is the opposite of that.

DHÛ-L-NÛN

MEDITATION

Anything of which we can conceive is not God. 'As the heavens are higher than the earth, so are God's thoughts higher than ours' (Isa. 55:9).

PRAYER

Teach us to adore You as *That of Which* nothing greater can be conceived, O God. Show us that You are Beyond every beyond, Ever-greater than any *thing* we can imagine.

Second Sight

When the Beloved appears, with what eye do I see Him? With His eye, not with mine, for none sees Him except Himself.

IBN 'ARABÎ

MEDITATION

'The eye with which we see God is the eye with which God sees us' (Meister Eckhart). In loving us, God is loving Himself - in, through, and *as* us.

PRAYER

Show us that we are blessed recipients of Your self-glorification, O God. Show us that we are created to become 'the praise of Your glory' (Eph. 1:12-14).

Unknowing

Praise to God who has given His creatures no way of attaining knowledge of Him except through their inability to know Him.

ABÛ BAKR

MEDITATION

We know God apophatically in a *Cloud of Unknowing*. 'Learned ignorance' is how we have a face-to-face encounter with God in the dark.

PRAYER

Lead us into the 'luminous darkness' where Your uncreated Light illumines our hearts, O God. Bring us, by way of contemplation, into Your Holy of Holies.

Wherever We Turn

Wherever you turn, there is the face of God.

QUR'ÂN

MEDITATION

Where can we go that God is not already there? 'If we ascend to heaven, God is there! If we make our beds in the depths of hell, God is there!' (Ps. 139:8).

PRAYER

You are the Hound of Heaven, from whose loving pursuit we can never escape, O God. Show us that if we cannot see You everywhere, we will find You nowhere.

Elusive Otherness

Whether one is inclined to evil or good, whether one is an inmate in prison or a monk in a monastery, from the point of view of 'form,' everyone is other than He, but from the point of view of Reality, everything is He and none other than He.

JÂMÎ

MEDITATION

Nothing exists that is not 'of God'. Creation is the extension of God's own Godself into that which is 'other' from God. Yet, is anything ever 'other' from God?

PRAYER

Teach us to revere creation as a sacramental expression of Your divine Life, O God. Remind us that what You have created, we must not call common (Acts 10:15).

I Am, therefore It Is

The existence of the beggar is His existence, and the existence of the sick is His existence ... There is none but He in the world of existence.

IBN 'ARABÎ

MEDITATION

Existence is an act of God who is Pure Act (*Actus Purus*). Existence is also an act of divine Love, since *Pure Act* is also *Pure Love* (1 Jn. 4:8).

PRAYER

Grant us an intuition of pure being, O God. Show us that 'there is something rather than nothing' because everything about You is creative Love.

God Alone

The secret of all created things, both outward and inward, is clear - you do not see, in this world or the next, anything except God.

IBN 'ARABÎ

MEDITATION

God is 'all in all' - not only at the end of time (1 Cor. 15:28), but from all eternity. God cannot become, or accomplish, anything that God was not, or did not do, since before time began.

PRAYER

Grant us a sense of our eternal identity in You, O God. Impact us with the realization that before we were conceived in our mothers' wombs, You knew us (Jer. 1:5).

Show Yourself!

I was a hidden treasure, and I desired to be known, so I created the world.

HADÎTH

MEDITATION

God creates us to manifest His image and likeness in the world. We are living icons of God's inexpressible Presence.

PRAYER

Enflame us with Your divine Presence, O God. Make us incandescent filaments of Your ineffable glory.

Diabolos

Things lie hidden in their opposites, but for the existence of opposites, the Adversary would have no manifestations.

AL-ALAWÎ

MEDITATION

Evil divides, but love unites. God is found in the coincidence of opposites (*coincidentia oppositorum*) where diversity and distinction remain, but division is overcome.

PRAYER

Transport us beyond the world of antinomies and antagonisms, O God. Deliver us into Your divine Embrace where dialectics and diatribes go to die.

Unquenchable Thirst

Whoever has fallen into the ocean of God's Oneness grows thirstier every day. His thirst will never be appeased because he has a thirst for truth that can only be quenched by the Real.

ABÛ SAʿÎD IBN ABÎ-L-KHAYR

MEDITATION

Our thirst for God is unquenchable, our hunger for God insatiable. Seated at the Wedding Feast of God, we can, without cost, eat and drink to our hearts' content (Isa. 55:1).

PRAYER

For those who trust in You, 'the jar of meal is never spent, the pitcher of oil never fails', O God(1 Kgs. 17:16). Give us Your sustenance always (Jn. 6:34; 4:15)!

Aseity

We and Thou are not separate from each other, but we need Thee, whereas Thou do not need us.

JÂMÎ

MEDITATION

Strictly speaking, God does not need us. At the same time, it has *pleased* God never to be without us for the praise of His glory (Eph. 1:12-14).

PRAYER

Show us our dignity as Your adopted children, O God (Gal. 4:5-6). Show us that, though You do not need us, Your delight is to make Your home with us (Rev. 3:20: 21:3).

Alpha and Omega

He is the One without oneness, and the Single without singleness. He is the very existence of the First, and the very existence of the Last, the very existence of the Outward, and the very existence of the Inward. So, there is no first nor last, no outward nor inward, except Him, without these becoming Him, or Him becoming them.

IBN ʿARABÎ

MEDITATION

We are one with God without confusion, and we are completely 'other' from God. This is a 'great Mystery' (Eph. 1:9) of divine co-inherence: we are asymmetrically united with God as branch to Vine (Jn. 15:5).

PRAYER

Reveal our blessed dependence upon You, O God. Show us that the epitome of Your transcendence is to fill the world with Your divinizing Presence.

Change of Focus

My servant does not draw near to Me by works of devotion, until I love him; and, when I love him, I am the eye by which he sees, and the ear by which he hears.

HADÎTH QUDSÎ

MEDITATION

'We love, because God first loved us' (1 Jn. 4:19). Those who know the predilective love of God can say, 'It is no longer I who live, but God who lives in me' (Gal. 2:20).

PRAYER

Effect within us a divine synergy, O God. Unite us so fully with Yourself that when others see us, they see You, and when they hear us, they hear You (Lk. 10:16; Acts 9:4).

All in All

Those who regard all things as determined by God, turn to God in everything.

NÛRÎ

MEDITATION

Gratitude and faith come naturally to those who know God as the Source and Satisfaction of their every desire. Childlike trust comes naturally when we apprehend God as the *Alpha* and *Omega* of our existence.

PRAYER

Open us to the utter gratuity of all that is, O God. Arrest us with the uncanniness of creation such that our souls sing for joy continually in Your Presence.

Nameless

He who has no name appears by whatever name you will call Him.

DÂRÂ SHIKÔH

MEDITATION

God's Name is unpronounceable (Ex. 3:14) because God is 'without being' as we understand being. Still, God is 'near to all who call upon Him' (Ps. 145:18), regardless of what Name we choose to call Him.

PRAYER

Hear the cry of our prayer, O God (Ps. 86:6). Show us that You Who are 'far above every name' (Eph. 1:21) draw near to those who call upon You, regardless of how they name You.

The Beloved and I

I am He whom I love, and He whom I love is I. We are two spirits dwelling in one body, and if you see me, you see Him; and if you see Him, you see us both.

AL-HALLAJ

MEDITATION

God is never without us, and we are never without God, even though God has no need of us, and we depend entirely on God. We are, by God's grace, the human faces of the ever-living God.

PRAYER

Show us that in You 'we live and move and have our being' (Acts 17:28), O God. Make us worthy of being living theophanies of Your divine Love.

Printed in the United States
by Baker & Taylor Publisher Services